YOU'RE HIRED!

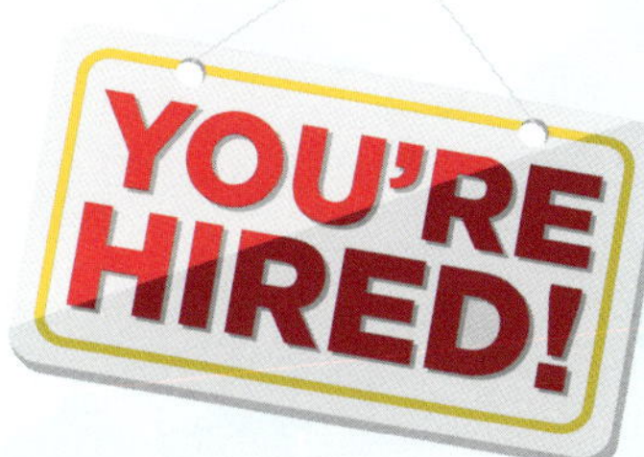

I Want to Start a LAWNCARE BUSINESS

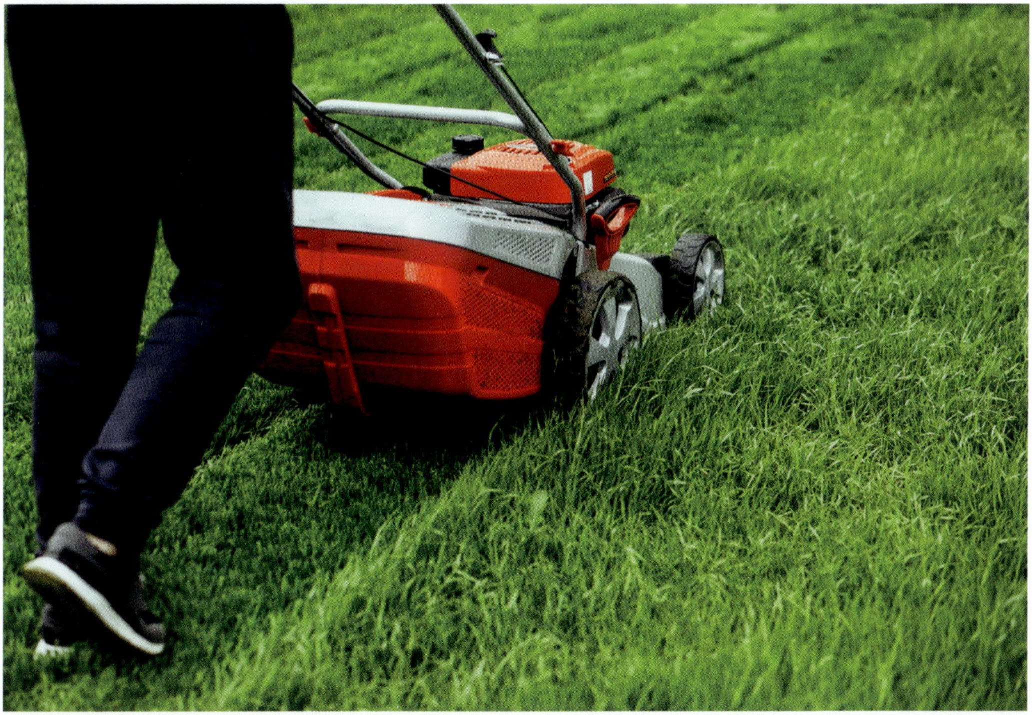

Mitchell Lane
PUBLISHERS

2001 SW 31st Avenue
Hallandale, FL 33009
www.mitchelllanepub.com

First Edition, 2025.
Author: Carla Mooney
Designer: Ed Morgan
Editor: Tammy Gagne

Series: You're Hired!
Title: I Want to Start a Lawncare Business

Hallandale, FL : Mitchell Lane Publishers, [2025]

Library bound ISBN: 978-1-68020-974-7
eBook ISBN: 978-1-68020-977-8

PHOTO CREDITS: Freepik.com

contents

CHAPTER ONE
Mowing and Mulching

Cameron wiped the sweat from his forehead. It was hot, but he would rather be outside than stuck indoors. He scanned the yard and admired the even stripes on the freshly cut lawn. He had started mowing lawns when he was only twelve years old. At first, it was one of his weekly chores at home. Then, he started cutting a few yards for neighbors on his street. Now, he had a list of customers that kept him busy from spring to fall.

Today, he was working at Mrs. Tyler's house. After mowing, Cameron loaded the lawn mower back into his pickup truck and grabbed his trimmer. He walked around the property with the tool. He used it to cut grass near the house and in other areas the mower could not reach. Then, he lifted his leaf blower and used it to remove grass clippings from the driveway, sidewalks, and back patio.

As he finished, Mrs. Tyler came out of the house and waved at him. “Cameron!” she called.

“Does everything look okay, Mrs. Tyler?” he asked.

She nodded. “Yes, it looks great as usual. I wanted to talk to you about **mulch**. When will you be available to mulch the flower beds?” she wanted to know.

Cameron thought for a moment. “I'm pretty busy for the rest of this week, but I could probably schedule it for one day early next week if that works for you,” he said.

Mrs. Tyler smiled. “Great, I'll have the mulch delivered on Monday. That way, it will be here when you can come over,” she said. “See you next week,” She waved again and went back into the house.

Cameron loaded the rest of his equipment into the pickup truck. Getting to his clients was easier since he had gotten his driver's license. Before that, his parents had driven him and his equipment to customers. He grabbed his phone and opened the calendar app. He added the mulching job to next week’s schedule.

Mowing and Mulching

A lawncare worker spreads fall leaves in a garden bed. The leaves provide essential minerals to the soil. The leaves also protect young plants from cold.

The lawncare business kept Cameron busy after school and during the summer, but he enjoyed it. Although mowing lawns was his primary job, there were different things to do every day. Some customers wanted him to mulch flower beds. Others wanted help planting small trees and shrubs. A few customers even hired him to help them with patio projects.

With the money he earned, Cameron bought a new lawnmower. He also added a few new lawncare tools to his collection. He hoped to hire a few friends as employees next summer.

WINTER Services

In many regions, lawncare is seasonal. Grass and shrubs stop growing in the winter. To earn money throughout the year, many lawncare businesses offer winter services. They remove snow with a shovel or snowblower. Some businesses set up holiday lights. Others remove leaves or clean gutters for customers.

Building a Lawncare Business

Sixteen-year-old Zach Cox runs his own lawn-mowing company called Zach's Lawncare. Cox's business in Ohio has grown from fifteen customers to almost fifty in the past two years. In addition to mowing lawns and performing other lawncare tasks, Cox also does maintenance jobs such as power washing driveways for his customers.

Cox plans to grow his business into a full-time job when he finishes school. "I love doing this. I feel like I'm going to be doing this for the rest of my life," he told Charles Payne on the Fox Business series *Making Money*. "Starting out so young, it's just something I've always loved, and that's why I've made it into an actual business."

CHAPTER TWO

A Job in Lawncare

Every spring and summer, teens nationwide fire up lawnmowers and get paid for the work they do. For those who like working outside, a job in lawncare can be ideal. Many homeowners hire other people to care for their lawns, gardens, and landscaping.

Cutting the Lawn

Most lawncare jobs start with mowing lawns. Growing grass should be cut regularly. It will grow faster and must be cut more often when there has been a lot of rain.

Teens who cut grass typically have a list of customers. They often mow their customers' lawns on a weekly schedule. Some teens use a push mower to cut lawns. Others use a riding mower.

Fifteen-year-old Joe Parsons from Farragut, Tennessee, started mowing lawns using his family's equipment. During an interview with WATE, his father recalled, "I handed him my push mower, and I gave him my blower. He went out and got a yard or two, and that's where it all began." Soon, Parsons's brothers, Shae and Landon, joined him in working on lawns. The siblings focus on making yards look great and getting gardens in good shape.

Age Requirements

Some states have a minimum age to operate a lawn mower. In states such as Georgia, North Carolina, Virginia, and Maryland, a person must be at least twelve years old to use a push mower. They must be at least sixteen to operate a riding mower. Teens interested in starting a lawncare business should check the age requirements for their state.

chapter TWO

Regular shrub trimming encourages new growth. It also gets rid of any dead or dying branches.

Homeowners appreciate their excellent work. Kim and Janis Wold are among these satisfied customers. The Wolds told WATE, "I'm sure with the job skills they've learned, it's going to carry over into adulthood."

In addition to mowing the grass, a lawncare worker will often trim grass that grows next to a wall or tree. Once all the cutting is finished, a lawncare worker may use a rake to collect and remove grass clippings. They can also use a leaf blower or broom to sweep grass clippings off driveways and sidewalks.

Other Lawncare Services

Many lawncare workers perform other yard services as well. Bushes and trees also need regular care and maintenance. Lawncare workers trim bushes and hedges yearly. In the spring, they may clear brush that has built up over the winter months. In the fall, they may rake or blow leaves off the lawn.

Sometimes, lawncare workers work on special projects for customers. They may remove old plantings and add new flowers or bushes. They may apply lawn **fertilizers** or plant new grass. In the spring, workers often spread mulch in garden beds. Some customers hire lawncare workers to power wash driveways and patios.

Lawncare workers keep their customers' yards looking good. They mow lawns, trim bushes, and collect clippings. For teens who like being outside and getting their hands dirty, lawncare can be a great way to make money.

In the spring, lawncare workers prepare gardens for planting. They maintain gardens throughout the growing season.

CHAPTER THREE

Traits for Success

Lawncare can be an excellent job for people who do not want to work inside behind a desk or a counter. People who are successful in lawncare usually love being outdoors. They enjoy getting their hands dirty. And they feel pride in creating and maintaining a beautiful outdoor space.

Active and Physical

Lawncare is physical work. People who do lawncare spend a lot of time on their feet. Many workers push lawnmowers across large yards. They load equipment into a car or truck and then unload it at each customer's location. They carry weed wackers and leaf blowers. They get down on their knees to spread mulch and **edge** gardens.

To do this job, lawncare workers must be in good physical shape. They must be able to spend hours at a time on their feet. Strength is needed to lift heavy equipment and carry bags of mulch. Workers must also be flexible enough to reach and bend.

Knowledge of Lawncare

To succeed, teens should understand how to care for lawns, gardens, and bushes. Beyond basic mowing, knowing how to trim and **prune** bushes is helpful. Understanding how fertilizers work and how to apply them is also beneficial.

A knowledge of basic plant care is also helpful in a lawncare business. Plants often have different sunlight, soil, and water needs. Knowing how to grow and maintain garden and yard plantings is important. Knowledge of pests and diseases that affect lawns, plants, trees, and bushes can also be helpful in lawncare.

Lawncare workers are careful not to prune trees too much. Over-pruning can damage a tree.

Lawncare workers must also be able to operate mowers, trimmers, leaf blowers, and other equipment. They should know how to maintain equipment to keep it performing at a high level. And when equipment breaks down, knowing how to fix it is also a valuable skill.

People and Communication Skills

To build a successful lawncare business, a person must do more than care for lawns and gardens. Lawncare workers need to have strong communication skills. Each week, workers talk to customers. The workers must be able to communicate effectively and listen to customers' needs.

Excellent customer service is key to keeping homeowners happy. Bryan Clayton is the founder of GreenPal, an online lawncare ordering service. He told *NerdWallet*, "Most customers have to deal with **shoddy** and unprofessional competitors. Creating a successful landscaping business is almost easy if you simply answer the phone when your customer calls, return their voicemails promptly, and do the work that you agree to with your **clientele**."

A lawncare worker uses a riding mower to cut a customer's lawn. Lawncare workers discuss scheduling for regular mowing with their customers.

chapter THREE

Financial Skills

Entrepreneurs should learn basic financial skills to keep track of their business transactions. They will need to record money earned as income. They should keep track of the money they pay for expenses such as gas or bags. They can record their income and expenses in a spreadsheet or a bookkeeping program.

Satisfied customers will often become long-term customers. They may recommend a lawncare business to neighbors and friends or post good online reviews. Positive reviews and word-of-mouth recommendations can bring in many new customers.

Business Skills

Starting and running a business is a lot of work. Successful business owners are organized. They know how to manage their time effectively. Lawncare workers create a schedule and stick to it. They finish jobs when promised, which creates satisfied customers.

For a business to succeed, people must know about it. Successful lawncare businesses know how to **market** themselves. They get the word out about their services. And they show potential customers why they are different from the competition.

Sometimes, the best way to learn is to work with a **mentor**. Spend time with other lawncare and landscaping professionals. Work for a lawncare business to learn basic skills on the job. Take classes in business management. Learn new skills to continue this path to success.

CHAPTER FOUR

How to Get Started

Starting a lawncare business is a great way to earn money. Many teens use lawnmowers and garden equipment their parents already own. Others save or borrow money from their parents to buy their own lawn mowers. With just a few steps, a teen can start building a lawncare business.

Services, Equipment, and Hours

First, teens need to decide what services they will offer. Beyond mowing, additional services might include weeding, mulching, edging, trimming, and planting. Teens should think about both what they already know how to do and what they are willing to learn. They should also consider what equipment they will need for the services they choose to provide.

Next, teens should organize their equipment and supplies. Make sure all the necessary tools are available and working properly. Take care of any maintenance or repair before advertising services. For example, if the lawnmower needs a tune-up, get it done before agreeing to mow any lawns. Equipment and tools should be regularly inspected and kept in good working condition.

Teens also need to decide how many hours they plan to work. When making a schedule, consider school and other commitments. When advertising their lawn mowing services, middle schoolers Marin Kickbush and Appian Kitchen from Arlington, Virginia, were very specific with their schedule. They told the *Today Show* that their sign read, "Only available on weekends. Sometimes we will not be able to mow."

Teens must also know how they will get to each customer's location. Older teens can often drive themselves to a customer's house. Younger teens may need their parents to drive them. Teens Trevor Plante and Nico Montoya from Springfield, Massachusetts, built a bicycle-drawn trailer to carry their lawncare equipment. Before the trailer, they relied on their parents to get to jobs. "We were unable to do as many jobs as we could handle because we had to wait for transportation," Trevor told the *MassLive* website.

How to Get Started

Planning is an important first step in starting a lawncare business. Before they start, teens should make decisions about services, pricing, equipment, and transportation.

Paying Taxes

If teens earn enough money, they will have to pay taxes. Teens making over $400 (income minus expenses) must file a **tax return**. They are responsible for paying self-employment taxes on earnings over $400. They may owe income taxes if their earnings exceed the standard deduction.

Set Prices

One of the most important parts of any business is deciding how much money to charge. Setting prices for mowing lawns and other lawncare services depends on a few factors. These factors include the customer's location, the size of the project, and how long it will take to finish. Teens should also find out how much people in the area usually pay for lawncare. The cost of supplies, fuel, and equipment should also be considered.

Some lawncare workers charge by the hour. Others charge by the yard. For larger projects, some workers charge a daily fee. Many lawncare businesses figure out how much they want to make per hour. They use that amount to set their prices. An example is a teen who wants to make $25 per hour. If a new customer's yard will take about two hours to mow, the teen should charge $50 to cut the lawn.

Get Customers

Finding customers can be the most challenging part of starting a lawncare business. Mowing lawns for family and friends can be a great way to build a customer list. These people can recommend the lawncare business to people they know who might also be interested. This type of word-of-mouth advertising is one of the best ways to find new customers.

Posting on social media is another way to advertise a lawncare business. Many neighborhoods and communities have Facebook groups. Teens can join these groups and post about lawncare services.

Some teens create professional-looking flyers and business cards to advertise their lawncare services. They hand out flyers and cards to people they know. They also post them on bulletin boards at local businesses, schools, and churches, with approval. The more a business advertises its services, the more opportunities it will have to find new customers.

Business License

Requirements for a business license vary by city, county, and state. Teens should contact their local officials to learn what type of business license they will need to start a lawncare business in their city or town.

CHAPTER FIVE

A Typical Day on the Job

Every day in lawncare is different. No two customers, yards, or gardens are exactly the same. The variety is one of the reasons why many people enjoy working in lawncare.

During breaks from school, the day of a lawncare worker usually starts early. Lawncare workers check the schedule to see what customers and projects are planned. They check the necessary equipment to make sure it is working properly. They add fuel to lawn mowers. Then, they head to the first job.

chapter FIVE

Lawncare work changes day by day. Some days, workers mow the lawns of several customers. On other days, they may spend the entire day at one customer's house spreading mulch in garden beds. Other times, they might prune trees, trim hedges, or pull weeds. In the spring, they plant flowers. In the fall, they rake and bag leaves.

Rainy Days

Rainy days can disrupt a lawncare schedule. While teens can mow lawns in light rain, mowing can become dangerous in heavy downpours. Also, electrical equipment should not be used in the rain. Instead, teens can use manual tools for weeding, trimming bushes, and spreading mulch in the rain.

A Typical Day on the Job

In the fall, a lawncare worker rakes leaves that have fallen from nearby trees. Fall clean-up activities such as raking leaves are a typical part of a lawncare worker's job.

chapter FIVE

A lawncare worker performs maintenance on a lawnmower. Regular maintenance of lawnmowers and other lawncare equipment keeps these tools working properly and ready for the next job.

When they have finished a job, lawncare workers meet with customers. They make sure the customer is satisfied. They deliver the bill and collect the payment.

Lawncare workers also meet with new customers. The workers explain the lawncare services in this meeting and go over pricing. Customers can describe what services they want done and what their expectations are. If a customer hires the lawncare service, the worker will add the property to the schedule.

At the day's end, the worker unloads equipment at home. They perform any needed maintenance on the equipment. This way, everything will be ready for the next day's jobs.

Future Careers

Starting a lawncare business can be a stepping stone to a future career for teens. Some teens decide to grow their lawncare businesses. Others use their experiences to start careers as landscape professionals, designers, or architects.

Landscape designers plan landscaping projects. They work with customers to create a design plan for a space. When creating the plan, the designer considers the customer's style and budget. Designers choose plants that grow well in the local soil and climate. Landscape designers often earn an associate's or bachelor's degree in plant-related majors such as botany or horticulture. Paul Corsetti is a professional landscape designer. He told *The Spruce* website, "Learning your plants and how to work with difficult soils is crucial if you want to become a landscape designer. You need to recognize what type of soil you're designing gardens for." Some designers also earn industry **certifications**.

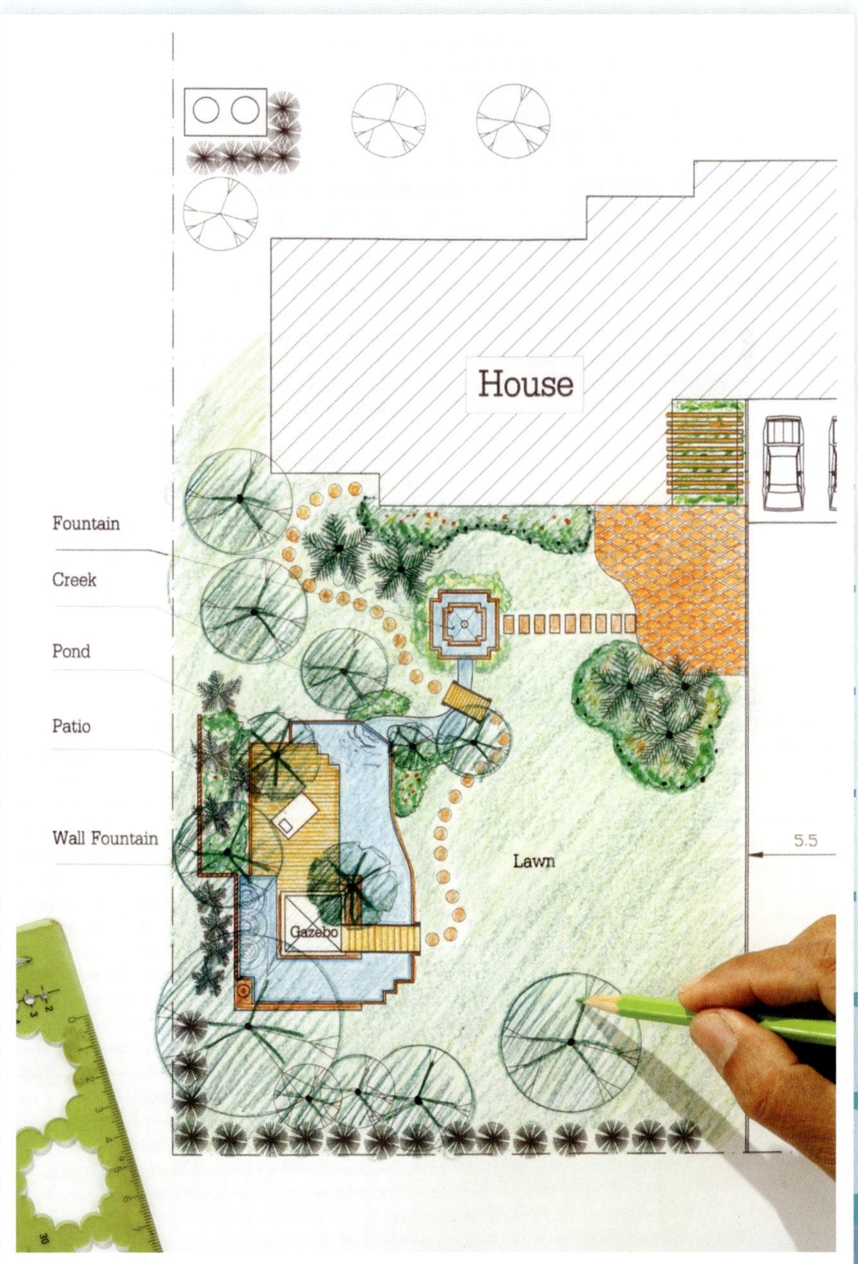

Some lawncare workers go on to become landscape designers. These professionals use their knowledge of plants and soils to design outdoor spaces for customers.

chapter FIVE

A Typical Day on the Job

Teens can start a lawncare business with a lawn mower, a few garden tools, and a little creativity. A lawncare business can be a great fit for teens who like being outdoors. They can earn money and valuable business experience close to home.

glossary

certifications
Official documents confirming that a person has certain skills and knowledge

clientele
The customers of a business

edge
To cut a border in a lawn between grass and a sidewalk, driveway, or garden

entrepreneurs
People who open and run their own businesses

fertilizers
Chemical or natural substances added to soil to make grass and plants grow better

market
To draw attention to a business, product, or service

mentor
An experienced and trusted advisor

mulch
A material such as decaying leaves or bark that is spread over a garden to improve and protect soil

prune
To cut off part of a plant to make it grow better

shoddy
Producing low-quality work

tax return
A yearly report sent to the government about income for the purpose of paying taxes

find out MORE

PRINT

Mooney, Carla. **You're Hired!** *I Want to Work in Food Service*. Hallandale, FL: Mitchell Lane Publishers, 2024.

Liu, Janet. *Making and Saving Money*. New York, NY: Scholastic, 2024.

Sheeks, Dan. *First to a Million: A Teenager's Guide to Achieving Early Financial Freedom*. Denver, CO: BiggerPockets Publishing, 2021.

ON THE INTERNET

Aebischer, Christine. "28 Business Ideas for Teens," *Nerd Wallet*, April 7, 2021.
https://www.nerdwallet.com/article/small-business/business-ideas-for-teens

Biz Kids.
https://bizkids.com

National Association of Landscape Professionals.
https://www.landscapeprofessionals.org

Anglin, Jesscia. "How to Make Money Doing Yardwork for Kids," *Kids' Money*, n.d. https://www.kidsmoney.org/kids/earning/yard-work.

Beaulieu, David. "How to Become a Landscape Designer," *The Spruce*, June 26, 2019. www.thespruce.com/how-to-become-a-landscape-designer-2132376.

Goldschein, Eric. "How to Start a Landscaping or Lawn Care Business," *Nerd Wallet*, October 22, 2020. www.nerdwallet.com/article/small-business/how-to-start-a-landscaping-business.

Hanson, Kait. "Kids' Brutally Honest Lawn Mowing Business Sign Shows the True Art of Setting Boundaries," *Today*, February 24, 2023. www.today.com/parents/family/funny-lawn-mowing-sign-rcna72166.

Ludden, Matt. "When Does Grass Start Growing?" *The Mower Shop*, April 27, 2022. https://themowershop.com/when-does-grass-start-growing/#:~:text=When%20the%20ground%20temperature%20reaches,these%20lawns%20are%20incredibly%20healthy.

Robbins, Carolyn. "Teens Launch Landscaping Business in Springfield's Forest Park," *Mass Live*, July 20, 2023. https://www.masslive.com/living/2023/07/teens-launch-landscaping-business-in-springfields-forest-park.html&subscribed=auth0%7C64ffb1b618caba463eba4ef3.

Schwab-Pomerantz, Carrie. "Does Your Teen Need to File a Tax Return?" *Charles Schwab*, March 15, 2022. https://www.schwab.com/learn/story/does-your-teen-need-to-file-tax-return.

Sisk, Andrew. "Mowing and Trimming a Lawn," *HGTV*, n.d. https://www.hgtv.com/outdoors/landscaping-and-hardscaping/lawns/mowing-and-trimming-a-lawn.

Stabile, Angelica. "Ohio Teen Grows Successful Lawncare Business from Ground Up: 'I Love Doing This.'" Fox *Business*, May 5, 2021. www.foxbusiness.com/money/ohio-teen-grows-successful-lawn-care-business-from-ground-up-i-love-doing-this.

Tejada, Katie. "8 Skills You Need to Have for a Landscaping Business," *Business Load*, October 5, 2020. https://www.businessload.com/run-grow-business/8-skills-you-need-to-have-for-a-landscaping-business.

Tucker, Lori. "11-Year-Old's Goal of Making $1,000 Turns into a Successful Lawncare Business," *WATE*, July 14, 2023. www.wate.com/news/positively-tennessee/teen-running-successful-business-with-his-brothers.

"A Typical Day Working Your New Landscaping Job," *Clean Cut Lawn & Landscape*, n.d. https://www.cleancutlandscape.net/2019/04/a-typical-day-working-your-new-landscaping-job.

index

about the author

Carla Mooney is the author of many books for young adults and children. She lives in Pittsburgh, Pennsylvania, with her husband and three children. As a teen, Mooney used a push mower to cut the lawn at her family home.